Santa at Night

Benton Robertson

M.D Habib

Benton is a determined boy with the biggest heart. He is the first to help, the first to ask questions, and the first to challenge you. His favorite color is blue, his favorite food is mac 'n cheese, and his favorite sport is hockey. In school, Benton loved Wonderful Writing which helped him to write his first book, Santa at Night.

To my kindergarten teachers, Mrs. K and Mrs. S., for two years of Wonderful Writing, and to my reading buddy, Evan, for inspiring me to create my first book.

To my Mommy, Daddy and big bro, Hudson for always helping and encouraging me.

"My family sticks to my heart" ~ Benny B!

SANTA

AT

NIGHT

HE

DELIVERS

PRESENTS

SANTA

AT

NIGHT

HE

DELIVERS

CANDY

SANTA
AT
NIGHT
HE
DELIVERS
TOYS

SANTA

AT

NIGHT

HE

DELIVERS

JOY

SANTA
AT
NIGHT
HE
DELIVERS
HOCKEY
EQUIPMENT

SANTA
AT
NIGHT
HE
DELIVERS
STUFFY'S

SEARCH 'N FIND

Where is Santa

Can you find Mrs. Claus

Who is "the most famous reindeer of all"

How many Elves can you find

Count the reindeer

Whose pants are the same color as a candy cane

MERRY CHRISTMAS SANTA

I

HOPE

YOU

LIKE

THE

MILK

AND

COOKIES